SUPER
SIMPLE
ONE POUND
BUDGET FAMILY MEALS

SUPER SIMPLE ONE POUND BUDGET FAMILY MEALS

Tasty Family Meals For Less

Copyright © Bell & Mackenzie Publishing Limited 2018

ISBN 978-1-912511-78-5

DISCLAIMER

CONTENTS

FISH   **83**

INTRODUCTION

Super Simple *One Pound Budget Family Meals will introduce you to a new way to shop for and cook simple but tasty family meals that will get nods of approval from the family and won't burn a hole in your shopping budget.*

Family meal planning can be a tricky and expensive affair - a never-ending cycle of chicken and minced beef on the menu with less then enthusiastic responses from the kids. You go into auto-pilot mode with repeat ordering from favourites on your weekly shopping list without any real thought or planning into what's going to be served up during the busy week ahead. Worse are the fast food 'easy back-up meals' of beans, sausage rolls & tomato ketchup that you can rustle up in no time. These are always popular with the kids but they are lacking in the nutritional department leaving you feeling guilty for not providing a more wholesome option. You're conscious of the monotony of weekly food shopping & preparation and painfully aware that this increasingly expensive cost is made worse by the inevitable waste of unused items that are thrown out each week.

Sound familiar?

Super Simple One Pound Budget Family Meals will introduce you to a new way to shop for and cook simple but tasty family meals that will get nods of approval from the family and won't burn a hole in your shopping budget. In fact you'll notice a big difference in how much you spend. Our smart shopping tips and even smarter cooking will enable you to create delicious meals for a family of four for approximately £1 per head. With a little planning and clever choices you'll be able to create lovely, simple dishes that make the best of fresh ingredients, use up what's in your fridge and store cupboard and stop wastage. It's a win-win approach to family meal planning.

LET'S GET STARTED!

SHOP SMART

You'll likely have heard this term before and attributed it to seeking out the cheaper 'own brand' supermarket products rather than the premium options, but that's only part of the equation to solving the problem of family meal budgeting.

There are a number of ways in which you can slash your weekly shopping budget with only a little more effort that will pay you dividends not only in the change left in your purse each week but in the rewards you will reap by serving up tasty & healthy meals to your family.

CONSIDER CHANGING WHERE YOU SHOP

If one of the major supermarket chains is your usual preference, try changing to one of the budget stores for a few weeks. You'll notice a big difference in the price of many products; often due to the lack of expensive and unnecessary packaging – usually in the fresh produce aisles. While a change of supermarket might add an extra few minutes shopping time because you are unfamiliar with the layout of the store, you'll soon become acquainted and will often find some new inspiration too. The 'no-nonsense' approach from budget supermarkets means lower-costs.

LOOK AT THE SUPERMARKETS' 'OWN BRAND' OR 'EVERYDAY' RANGES

By checking the package information you will often find that there is little or no difference in the ingredients – you'll find lots of savings can be made on everyday products such as tinned chopped tomatoes and pasta.

USE STORE LOYALTY CARDS

Nearly every supermarket has their own scheme offering 2 for 1 deals or money off. Make the most of offers but don't buy items you are unlikely to use just because they are on offer! Keep your loyalty card on your key ring so you don't miss collecting your points. Also many stores regularly offer vouchers in newspapers and magazines. Don't be ashamed to cut them out and use them for money off at the till.

CONSIDER VEGETARIAN OPTIONS

Meat can be expensive. While there are cheaper cuts to be bought, cooking without meat can be cheaper and sometimes healthier. We've included some delicious vegetarian options that will open your eyes to a different way of creating low-cost but tasty meals.

USE CHEAPER CUTS OF MEAT

Don't be intimidated by cuts of meat that you may not be familiar with. Often these can be just as delicious as your preferred cut using an alternative method of cooking (e.g. slow cooking). Cuts such as beef brisket or shin, lamb chump and pork belly can all make you savings. Similarly using fish such as pollock, hake or whiting can be a much cheaper and a sustainably preferable substitute for haddock or cod.

STRIP BACK EXPENSIVE INGREDIENTS

Often cookbooks have a long list of expensive and obscure ingredients that can end up spoiling and gathering dust if you don't have other recipes or meal ideas to use them up with. Whilst these ingredients can make a difference to a dish and enhance its flavour, often stripping them out or replacing them with an alternative can make a significant difference to the cost without losing the flavour. For example:

- A traditional lasagne usually asks for mozzarella cheese, cheaper cheddar cheese (or whatever is on offer on the cheese counter) will do the job just as well.
- Does the recipe really need chipotle paste? Wouldn't a few crushed chilli flakes do the job just as well.

Our recipes are based on this principle of keeping things simple and inexpensive without compromising on taste. We're creating honestly good £1 family meals not fussy Masterchef rated fine dining.

With this new simplified approach to cooking we'd also encourage you as much as possible to experiment with ingredients. If you find you are missing a specific herb, try substituting with another – you'll often find the results are still delicious. Flexibility and confidence is the key.

Most of our recipes use 'repeat' ingredients. This is the clever way to avoid waste. What you might not use in one recipe can go back in the fridge and be used in another. There are some staple store cupboard ingredients you will need but you will likely have most of these already.

COOKING FOR ONE OR TWO?
Our meals are designed for four people but you can easily portion and refrigerate or freeze our meals to use on another day. This is a great way to plan and keep costs down. Alternatively you just cut down on the quantities when preparing.

ENJOY COOKING FROM SCRATCH
Our super simple £1 family meals mean you can really keep track of what you're eating. Freshly prepared ingredients avoid the need for expensive and processed jars of 'convenience' foods full of salt and preservatives. You can be happy in the knowledge that your meals are transparent and free from unnecessary flavourings and additives.

ECONOMICS
Purchasing ingredients for family meals means you will likely have to buy larger packs than you might use.

Each is based around meals for four that cost roughly £1 a head, although the £1 cost price can only be achieved if you use the entirety of all the ingredients across a number of recipes.

For e.g. a pancake recipe may use ingredients including 75g flour and an egg. Obviously you can't buy ingredients in these specific quantities, so buying all the ingredients for pancakes may initially cost you £3-4 but the idea is you build up a store cupboard of ingredients and use these repeatedly to achieve budget £1 meals.

Basic store cupboard ingredients are not included in the £1 per head costing; staples like salt and pepper, cooking oil and dried herbs. You're likely to already have these to hand but if you don't, a little upfront expense in stocking up with these will reap benefits and they will store well for a long time. You can make clever choices with your store cupboard ingredients – you don't need extra virgin olive oil for cooking for example and store branded jars of herbs are much cheaper then the well known spice brands.

We do our best across the recipes to repeat ingredients to make sure you aren't left with lots of useless half used herbs & spices etc. Once you get into the groove of budget cooking you 'll soon find that you are regularly on a cycle of £1 per head meals and using all the ingredients you have in your fridge and store cupboard with little or no waste.

Obviously food prices will fluctuate depending on the season and market forces but with smart shopping and paying attention to price changes you should be able to maintain your budget meals throughout the year.

We hope you enjoy creating our delicious low-cost £1 budget family meals.

ABOUT COOKNATION

CookNation is the leading publisher of innovative and practical recipe books for the modern, health conscious cook.

CookNation titles bring together delicious, easy and practical recipes with their unique no nonsense approach - making cooking for diets and healthy eating fast, simple and fun. With a range of #1 best-selling titles - from the innovative 'Skinny' calorie-counted series, to the 5:2 Diet Recipes collection - CookNation recipe books prove that 'Diet' can still mean 'Delicious'!

To browse all CookNation's recipe books visit www.bellmackenzie.com

 CookNation

SUPER SIMPLE

One Pound
MEAT
Recipes

Peanut Butter Chicken

Ingredients

- 2 tbsp olive oil
- 8 chicken thigh fillets, quartered
- 1 garlic clove, crushed
- 1 tbsp curry powder
- 3 tbsp smooth peanut butter
- 400ml tin coconut milk
- 400g tin chopped tomatoes

Method

1 Heat the oil in a frying pan and brown the chicken in batches until they are golden. Put each thigh on a plate to one side as you brown the next.

2 Once all the thighs are browned gently sauté the garlic in the same pan for a couple of minutes.

3 Stir in the peanut butter, coconut milk and tomatoes, and bring to the boil for a moment.

4 Return the chicken to the pan, cover and simmer for 25-30 mins until the chicken is cooked through and the sauce is reduced by about half.

5 Divide into bowls and serve.

CHEF'S NOTE
Chicken thighs make a great budget meat option, they also happen to be the tastiest part of the bird. Buy in bulk to save on costs and freeze the rest until needed.

'Ikea' Meatballs & Mustard Mash

SUPER SIMPLE

Ingredients

- 1 piece of bread
- 500g pork or beef mince
- ½ onion
- 1 garlic clove
- 1 tbsp olive oil

- 1 tin condensed mushroom soup
- 500g potatoes, peeled & cubed
- 2 tsp mustard
- 2 tsp butter
- Splash of milk

Method

1 Whizz the bread in a food processor to make breadcrumbs.

2 Add the mince, onion and garlic to the food processor and pulse until everything is well combined.

3 Use your (wet) hands to form the mince into 12-16 evenly sized meatballs.

4 Heat the oil in a frying pan and brown the meatballs for 5 mins over a medium heat.

5 Stir in the mushroom soup along with half a tin of water.

6 Cover and simmer for 10-15 mins until the meatballs are cooked through and the soup has reduced to a thick-ish sauce.

7 Meanwhile cook the cubed potatoes in salted boiling water until tender.

8 Drain and mash with the mustard, butter and a splash of milk.

9 Season the meatballs and serve over the mustard mash.

CHEF'S NOTE
If you don't have any mustard in your store cupboard just leave it out of the mash.

Ragu Orzo

Ingredients

- 1 onion, finely chopped
- 2 garlic cloves
- 1 tbsp olive oil
- 400g minced beef
- 1 tin chopped tomatoes

- 250ml tomato passata
- 1 tsp dried mixed herbs
- 1 tbsp balsamic vinegar
- 350g orzo pasta
- Salt & pepper to taste

Method

1 Gently sauté the onion and garlic in the olive oil for a few minutes until softened. Add the beef and brown for a further 3-4 minutes.

2 Add the chopped tomatoes, passata, herbs & balsamic vinegar and simmer for 15 minutes to make a simple ragu.

3 Continue to cook the ragu while you boil the kettle and fill a saucepan with boiling water and a large pinch of salt.

4 Add the pasta and leave to cook until the orzo is tender.

5 As soon is the pasta is ready quickly drain and add to the ragu.

6 Combine really well, check the seasoning and serve.

CHEF'S NOTE
Orzo is a small traditional pasta that cooks more quickly than larger shapes. Feel free to substitute with an alternative if you like it.

SERVES 4

Cowboy Casserole

Ingredients

- 1 tbsp olive oil
- 1 onion, sliced
- 12 pork sausages
- 1 garlic clove, crushed

- 1 tin chopped tomatoes
- 2 tins mixed beans
- 1-2 tsp paprika

Method

1 Heat the oil in a large frying pan and gently cook the garlic, onion and sausages for 10 mins.

2 Add the chopped tomatoes and mixed beans to the pan along with the paprika.

3 Bring to a hard simmer. Cover and leave to gently simmer for 10-15 mins or until everything is cooked through and piping hot.

CHEF'S NOTE

Not everyone in the family may like mixed beans so you could also use baked beans in their place and it wouldn't cost you any more.

Beef Keema

Ingredients

- 300g rice
- 1 tbsp olive oil
- 500g beef mince
- 1 onion, chopped
- 2 garlic cloves, crushed
- 2 tbsp curry powder
- 1 tin chopped tomatoes
- 200g frozen peas

Method

1 Cook the rice in salted boiling water. When it's ready, drain and put to one side.

2 Meanwhile heat the oil in a deep frying pan and brown the mince.

3 After the mince has browned for a couple of minutes, remove from the pan, leaving the oil in the pan.

4 Sauté the onion and garlic in leftover oil for a few minutes until softened.

5 Add the mince back into the pan along with the curry powder. Combine well before adding the chopped tomatoes, peas and rice.

6 Cover and leave to gently simmer for 15-20 mins or until the tomato juice has reduced by at least half.

CHEF'S NOTE

You can easily pickup 500g lean beef mince for less than £2. If your budget can stretch to it a tin of coconut cream and some chopped coriander makes a great addition too.

Chicken & Spinach Risotto

SUPER SIMPLE

Ingredients

- 2 tbsp butter
- 1 onion, chopped
- 1 garlic clove, crushed
- 300g risotto rice

- 1½ lt chicken or veg stock
- 200g cooked shredded chicken
- Handful of spinach, chopped (or frozen peas works fine too)

Method

1 Gently heat the butter in a large frying pan and sauté the onion & garlic for a few minutes until softened.

2 Add the risotto and combine really well to coat the rice in oil.

3 One ladle at a time add the stock until each ladle of stock is absorbed by the risotto. Continue until the risotto is tender and the stock is absorbed.

4 Add the shredded chicken into to pan along with the chopped spinach and stir well.

5 Warm through for a few minutes until everything is piping hot before dividing into bowls to serve.

CHEF'S NOTE
Serve with grated Parmesan if you have it or try the pangritata on page 57.

19

Sweet Chilli Chicken Traybake

Ingredients

- 8 chicken thighs
- 3 tbsp sweet chilli sauce
- 75g cashew nuts

- 350g rice
- 2 tsp olive oil
- 2 eggs

Method

1 Pre-heat the oven to 200C/Gas 6.

2 Slash the flesh of the chicken thighs deeply with a knife.

3 Place the chicken in a bowl. Combine with the sweet chilli sauce then arrange on a baking tray and roast for about 30 mins until cooked through.

4 Meanwhile cook the rice in salted boiling water. Drain the rice and add to a frying pan with the olive oil already warming in it.

5 Add the cashew nuts to the baking try and cook for a further 5 minutes.

6 While the nuts are roasting turn up the heat on the rice and break the eggs into it. Stir-fry for a couple of minutes.

7 Serve the egg fried rice with the sticky chicken and some more sweet chilli sauce on the side.

CHEF'S NOTE
You could also add some onions and peas to the egg fried rice if you fancy.

Corned Beef Hash & Paprika Beans

SUPER SIMPLE

Ingredients

- 750g potato, peeled and chopped
- 2 tbsp olive oil
- 1 onion
- 1 tin corned beef, cut into cubes
- 1 tin baked beans
- 2 tsp paprika

Method

1 Cook the cubed potatoes in a pan of salted pan water. Cook for approx. 8 mins or until they begin to cook through.

2 Drain and allow them to steam off while you heat the oil in a non-stick frying pan.

3 Gently sauté the onion for a few minutes until golden.

4 Add the potatoes and corned beef, and use the back of the spatula to crush the potatoes down a little and combine into a large pattie.

5 Cook for 5 mins, then flip over to cook the other side until both sides are crispy & golden brown.

6 Meanwhile heat the baked beans in a saucepan along with the paprika for a few minutes.

7 Season a little and serve the hash with the paprika beans on the side.

CHEF'S NOTE
Corned beef is a classic budget meal. Add some chopped steamed greens too if you have any to hand.

21

Sweet Pork & Baked Gnocchi

Ingredients

- 1 pack gnocchi
- 2 tsp olive oil
- 4 pork loin steaks

- 3 tbsp sweet chilli sauce
- 1 bag shredded spring greens
- 1 tbsp butter

Method

1 Pre-heat the oven to 200°C/Gas6.

2 Combine together the gnocchi and oil and tip onto a baking tray.

3 Combine together the pork loin steaks with the sweet chilli sauce and place on a large flat baking tray lined with baking parchment.

4 Bake the pork chops for 10 minutes. Turn the chops over and add the gnocchi tray to the oven.

5 Cook both the pork and the gnocchi for 15-20 minutes or until the pork is cooked through and the gnocchi is crispy and golden brown.

6 Meanwhile cook the greens and combine with the butter.

7 Plate up the gnocchi and pork, pile the butter greens on the side to serve.

CHEF'S NOTE

A bag of shredded greens can cost as little as 50p. However feel free to buy whole veg and shred it yourself if you see a better bargain.

SERVES 4

Sweet Chicken Kebabs

SUPER SIMPLE

Ingredients

- 3 tbsp teriyaki sauce
- 1 tbsp olive oil
- 2 tbsp clear honey
- 4 boneless chicken thighs, cut into chunks
- 1 tin pineapple chunks, drained
- 2 red peppers, de-seeded & cut into chunks
- 4 pitta bread

Method

1 Soak 4 long wooden skewers in cold water for at least 20 minutes.

2 Pre-heat the grill.

3 Combine together the teriyaki sauce, oil, honey, chicken, pineapple & peppers in a large bowl.

4 Line a baking tray with foil.

5 Thread the coated chicken, pineapple & peppers onto the skewers.

6 Place on the lined baking tray and cook under the grill for about 15 mins or until the chicken is cooked through.

7 Serve straight away in pitta pockets.

CHEF'S NOTE
The combined sweetness of the honey, pineapple and teriyaki sauce usually make these kebabs a huge hit with the kids.

Satay Beef Pitta Pockets

Ingredients

- 1 slice bread
- 500g beef mince
- 4 tbsp peanut butter
- 1 tbsp ketchup
- 1 tsp marmite

- ½ onion
- 1 tsp curry powder
- 8 mini pitta bread
- 1 iceberg lettuce, shredded

Method

1 Pre-heat the oven to 200C/Gas6.

2 Whizz the bread in a food processor to make breadcrumbs.

3 Add the mince, peanut butter, ketchup, marmite, curry powder and onion to the food processor and pulse until everything is well combined.

4 Use your (wet) hands to form the mince into about 24 walnut sized meatballs.

5 Place the meatballs on a lined baking tray and cook in the oven for 15-20 minutes or until cooked through.

6 Serve in mini pitta breads with shredded lettuce.

CHEF'S NOTE
Serve this with extra peanut butter for dipping too if you like.

Mango Chutney Pork

SUPER SIMPLE

Ingredients

- 4 pork loin steaks, cubed
- 2 tbsp olive oil
- 4 tbsp mango chutney
- 2 tbsp medium curry powder
- 1 onion, sliced
- 300g rice
- 1 lime

Method

1 Place the pork and curry powder in a plastic bag and shake well so that every piece of pork is covered.

2 Place the rice on to cook in salted boiling water

3 Heat the oil in a frying pan and cook the pork and onions for 10-15 minutes or until cooked through.

4 Stir the mango chutney through the frying pan with the pork and cook for a few minutes more until sticky.

5 Drain the rice and serve the sticky pork piled over the top with a piece of lime on the side to add to your taste.

CHEF'S NOTE

Pork loin is a good budget meat but chicken thighs will work equally well for this recipe.

Chicken Noodle Stir-Fry

SERVES 4

Ingredients

- 500g chicken thighs, cubed
- 1 tbsp olive oil
- 4 tbsp teriyaki sauce
- 300g egg noodles
- 1 chicken stock cube
- 75g sugar snap peas
- Handful of peanuts, chopped

Method

1 Heat the oil in a frying pan and cook the chicken for 10-15 minutes or until cooked through.

2 Stir the teriyaki sauce through the frying pan and cook on a gentle heat for a few minutes more until sticky.

3 Meanwhile cook the noodles in boiling water (with a stock cube crumbled in) until the noodles are tender. Just before draining add the sugar snap peas for the last 30 seconds of cooking.

4 Drain the noodles & peas and add to the frying pan.

5 Toss well and serve in shallow bowls with peanuts sprinkled over the top.

CHEF'S NOTE
You could also use hoisin sauce or sweet chilli sauce in place of the teriyaki.

Spicy Eastern Lamb Wraps

SUPER SIMPLE

Ingredients

- 500g lamb mince
- ½ -1 tsp chilli flakes (to suit your own taste)
- 2 tsp curry powder
- 1 tbsp olive oil
- Small tub Greek yoghurt
- 1 red cabbage, shredded
- 4 tortilla wraps

Method

1 Flash-fry the mince in a frying pan with the olive oil, chilli flakes & curry powder.

2 When it's cooked, tip the mince onto the wraps with some shredded cabbage and a dollop of Greek yoghurt.

3 Sprinkle with a few more chilli flakes if you wish and fold the wraps.

4 Serve straight away.

CHEF'S NOTE
Lamb often isn't the cheapest of cuts but lean lamb mince makes a good economical option.

SERVES 4

Pesto Steak

Ingredients

- 800g new potatoes
- 200g frozen peas
- 2 tbsp green pesto

- 200g beef frying steak, sliced into strips
- 1 tbsp olive oil

Method

1 Halve the new potatoes and cook in salted boiling water for approx. 15 minutes or until tender. Put the peas in with the potatoes for the last few minutes of cooking.

2 Drain and put to one side while you heat the olive oil in a deep frying pan or wok.

3 Flash fry the steak for a couple of minutes in the oil then pile in the potatoes, peas and pesto.

4 Stir-fry until everything is cooked through and piping hot.

5 Divide into bowls and serve.

CHEF'S NOTE
This is makes a fantastic filling meal. Increase the amount of beef steak if your budget can stretch to it.

Lamb & Pickled Onion Stew

SUPER SIMPLE

Ingredients

- 350g cubed lamb
- 1 tbsp olive oil
- 1 tsp dried mixed herbs
- 1 small jar silverskin pickled onions
- 2 tins chopped tomatoes
- 250ml boiling water
- 600g new potatoes, halved

Method

1 Pre-heat the oven to 180C/Gas5

2 In an oven-proof dish heat the oil on the hob and quickly brown the meat for a minute or two.

3 Drain the pickled onions and add to the pan along with the chopped tomatoes, dried herbs and potatoes.

4 Add 250ml of boiling water. Combine really well and place in the oven.

5 Cover and leave to cook for about 2 hours or until the sauce has reduced and everything is cooked through, tender and piping hot.

CHEF'S NOTE
Add a tsp of marmite to the casserole if you have some to hand.

Simple Superfast Lunchtime Noodles

Ingredients

- 4 eggs
- 1 tbsp curry powder
- 300g egg noodles
- 150g frozen peas

- Bunch of spring onions, sliced
- 1 tbsp olive oil
- 200g cooked ham

Method

1 Break the eggs into a bowl and whisk in the curry powder.

2 Cook the noodles in salted boiling water, adding the peas for the last couple of minutes of cooking.

3 When the noodles are tender, drain.

4 In the meantime heat the oil in a frying pan and sauté the spring onions.

5 Tip in the drained noodles & peas into the spring onions and increase the heat.

6 Add the eggs & ham and stir-fry for a few minutes until everything is cooked through and piping hot.

CHEF'S NOTE
Use cooked ham or salami any leftover cooked meat will work for these simple superfast curry noodles.

Bacon & Pea Salad

SUPER
SIMPLE

········· *Ingredients* ·········

- 4 large red onions, cut into 8 wedges
- 6 tbsp olive oil
- 200g frozen peas
- 1 tbsp red wine vinegar

- 1 tbsp Dijon mustard
- 8 slices of bacon
- 2 Romaine lettuces, shredded
- 1 crusty baguette

········· *Method* ·········

1 Pre-heat the oven to 220C/Gas 7.

2 Place the onion wedges in a bowl and combine with 2 tbsp of the olive oil.

3 Season with salt & pepper and tip the oily onions onto a baking tray and roast for 15 mins.

4 Meanwhile, cook the peas in boiling water for 2 mins, drain and put to one side.

5 Combine together the remaining olive oil, red wine vinegar and mustard to make a dressing.

6 Take the onions out of the oven. Turn them over and make some space for

the bacon. Place the onions and bacon back in the oven and cook for 10-12 mins or until the bacon is cooked through and the onions are tender.

7 Meanwhile arrange the lettuce and cooled peas in bowls.

8 Tear the bacon slices up a bit and pile the onions and bacon pieces onto the salad.

9 Drizzle the dressing all over and serve with pieces of crusty bread; which you could drizzled a little oil over too.

Homemade Chutney & Bacon Paninis

Ingredients

- 4 large tomatoes, chopped
- 1 onion, chopped
- 2 tbsp balsamic vinegar
- 1 tbsp sugar
- 8 slices of bacon
- 4 Panini rolls
- Shredded lettuce or salad leaves to serve

Method

1 First make the chutney by combining together the tomatoes, onion, vinegar & sugar in a saucepan over medium-low heat.

2 Cook, uncovered, stirring frequently, until thickened for about 10 to 15 minutes.

3 Meanwhile cook the bacon and get this into the Panini rolls along with the shredded lettuce.

4 Slather the warm chutney inside the Panini rolls and serve.

CHEF'S NOTE
If you have a sandwich toaster or grill use this to grill the Paninis for a few minutes before serving.

Barley & Gammon Casserole

SUPER SIMPLE

Ingredients

- 1 tbsp olive oil
- 2 onions, sliced
- 1 tsp mixed dried herbs
- 2 garlic cloves, finely chopped
- 300g pearl barley
- 6 carrots, chopped

- 1 tbsp Dijon mustard
- 1lt chicken stock
- 1 cabbage, shredded
- 300g gammon joint, cooked, chopped into small pieces

Method

1 Gently sauté the onions with the olive oil in a large saucepan on a medium heat.

2 Add the garlic and dried herbs and cook for a couple of minutes more.

3 Add the pearl barley, carrots, mustard & chicken stock.

4 Season well, cover and simmer for approx. 20 mins.

5 Add the cabbage & gammon and cook for a further 10 mins or until the pearl barley is tender and cooked through and the stock is mostly absorbed.

6 Divide into bowls and serve.

CHEF'S NOTE

Gammon joints make a fantastic cheap and versatile cooking ingredient. Buy a large joint to cook and you'll be able to use if for multiple meals.

Liver & Bacon dinner

Ingredients

- 800g potatoes, peeled & cubed
- 1 tbsp butter
- Splash of milk
- 4 rashers of bacon
- 2 tbsp plain flour
- 1 tsp paprika

- 400g lamb's livers, sliced
- 2 tbsp olive oil
- 1 onion, sliced
- 300ml beef stock
- 2 tbsp ketchup

Method

1 Cook the potatoes in salted boiling water. When they are tender drain and mash well with the butter and milk.

2 Meanwhile grill the bacon until it is very crisp and put to one side to cool before finely chopping it.

3 Combine the lamb's livers with the flour and paprika.

4 Heat the olive oil in a frying pan and brown the liver for a minute or two before setting aside.

5 Add the onions to the empty oily pan (add more oil if needed) and gently sauté for a couple of minutes.

6 Stir in stock and ketchup and bring to a hard simmer for 5 mins.

7 Put the liver back in the pan and cook for 2-3 mins or until the liver is cooked through.

8 Pile the liver onto mashed potatoes and sprinkle the bacon on top.

CHEF'S NOTE
Lambs livers are terrific value for money. They're not something we tend to eat these days but don't be put off. They taste fab.

SERVES 4

Bacon & Onion Quiche

······· *Ingredients* ·······

- 250g all-butter shortcrust pastry
- 150g bacon lardons
- 1 onion, chopped
- Large carton of double cream

- 150ml milk
- 2 large eggs + 2 egg yolks
- 150g grated cheddar

······· *Method* ·······

1 Pre-heat the oven to fan 180C/Gas 5.

2 Cook the pastry for 15 minutes in a lined 22cm loose-bottomed tart tin. Before cooking, prick it and weight it down – dried pulses work well for this. After 15 mins take it out of the oven.

3 Meanwhile, cook the lardons in a frying pan until very crispy.

4 Remove the bacon from the pan and use the left over oil to gently cook the onions. Cook the spring onions in the fat over a moderate heat for 1 minute until softened. Remove with slotted spoon and tip over the bacon.

5 In a glass bowl combine together the lardons, onions, cream, milk, eggs, egg yolks and grated cheese.

6 Pour this into the pastry case. Reduce the heat in the oven to 160C/Gas5 and cook for 30 mins or until the centre is 'set' and firm to the touch.

7 Remove from the oven and place on a cooling rack before slicing and serving.

CHEF'S NOTE
You could replace the bacon lardons for ham or if you've already cooked a gammon joint for any of the other recipes.

Devilled Kidneys

Ingredients

- 800g fresh pig's kidneys
- 2 tbsp olive oil
- 1 tbsp red wine vinegar
- 1 tbsp Worcestershire sauce
- 2 tbsp mustard
- 2 tsp paprika
- Small carton double cream
- 4 thick slices of bloomer bread, toasted

Method

1 Cut the kidneys into quarters and trim out the hard core inside.

2 Heat the oil in a large frying pan on high and add the kidneys, browning for a minute on each side.

3 Add the vinegar, Worcestershire sauce, mustard & paprika.

4 Combine well before adding the cream.

5 Allow to bubble away on the heat for a couple of minutes until the cream thickens.

6 Season well and serve on toasted bread.

CHEF'S NOTE
Pigs kidneys might not sound the most appealing ingredient for the family but these tender cuts are really excellent. Buy direct from your butcher if possible.

BBQ Sauce & Pork Belly Rolls

SUPER SIMPLE

Ingredients

- 4 tbsp ketchup
- 1 tbsp Worcestershire sauce
- 1 tbsp sugar
- 1 tbsp balsamic vinegar
- 1 tbsp soy sauce
- 1 tsp English mustard
- 1 clove garlic, crushed
- 500g pork belly joint
- 1 small tub coleslaw
- 4 Brioche burger buns

Method

1 Pre-heat the oven to 160C/Gas4.

2 In a glass bowl combine together the ketchup, Worcestershire sauce, sugar, balsamic vinegar, soy sauce, mustard & garlic to make a BBQ sauce.

3 Slice the pork belly joint into 8 thick slices and place on a large piece of kitchen foil.

4 Slather all the BBQ sauce over the pork, coating each side. Then loosely but completely cover with foil to make a foil dome over the top so that the air inside can circulate.

5 Place on a baking tray and roast for approx. 1hr 30 mins or until completely tender.

6 Load the BBQ pork slices in Brioche buns with coleslaw and serve.

CHEF'S NOTE
Brioche buns add a touch of luxury to this rustic lunch. You can pick up a pack for less than 80p.

Slow Cooked Pork & Beans

Ingredients

- 2 tins haricot beans, drained
- 1lt vegetable stock
- 2 onions, chopped
- 4 carrots, chopped

- 2 tbsp Dijon mustard
- 1 tbsp sugar
- 2 tbsp tomato puree
- 600g pork belly joint

Method

1 Pre-heat the oven to 160C/Gas 4.

2 Add all the ingredients to a flameproof casserole dish and bring to the boil.

3 Cover and cook in the oven for approx. 3hours or until the beans and pork are very tender.

4 Remove from the oven and place the pork joint on a chopping board. Cut into chunks and add back to the pot.

5 Combine well and serve in shallow bowls.

CHEF'S NOTE
Check the casserole about halfway through the cooking time and top up with hot water from the kettle if needed.

Creamy Tamarind Chicken

SUPER SIMPLE

····· *Ingredients* ·····

- 2 tbsp olive oil for the sauce
- 2 onions, sliced
- 4 garlic cloves
- 1 tsp ground ginger

- 1 tsp paprika
- 1 tin chopped tomatoes
- 250ml chicken stock
- 1 tbsp sugar
- 1 tin coconut milk

- 8 boneless chicken thighs
- 1 lime
- 3 tbsp olive oil, for frying
- 2 tbsp tamarind

····· *Method* ·····

1 First make the sauce by sautéing the onions, garlic, ginger and paprika in a frying pan for a few minutes until softened.

2 Add the tomatoes, stock, coconut milk & sugar and cook, uncovered, for approx. 20 mins or until the sauce has thickened and reduced a bit.

3 Pre-heat the oven to 180C/Gas 5.

4 Brown the chicken thighs in another frying pan with the olive oil for a minute or two each side.

5 Combine with the tamarind and place this in a casserole dish with the sauce.

6 Place in the oven and bake for 30 minutes or until everything is cooked through and piping hot.

CHEF'S NOTE

Tamarind is used in multiple recipes in this collection so don't worry about having some left over. Just store in the fridge until needed.

Classic Carbonara

.... Ingredients ....

- 350g farfalle
- 100g bacon lardons
- 2 tsp olive oil
- 2 eggs

- 1 small carton single cream
- 4 tbsp Parmesan style hard cheese, grated

.... Method ....

1 Cook the spaghetti in salted boiling water.

2 Meanwhile fry the lardons in oil until they are very crispy.

3 Remove from the pan, allow to cool then finely chop.

4 Gently beat the cream and eggs to together in a bowl.

5 When the pasta is ready, drain and return to the pan with the creamy eggs and bacon bits.

6 Stir well, really quickly over a low heat for just a minute or two to warm the cream.

7 Divide into bowls and cover with the grated cheese.

CHEF'S NOTE
Any type of pasta will do for this recipe. Add some peas to the cooking pasta too if you like.

Burns Night Broth

SUPER SIMPLE

Ingredients

- 1 tbsp olive oil
- ½ onion, sliced
- 200g potatoes, peeled & finely diced
- 200g carrots, peeled & finely diced
- 200g swede peeled & finely diced
- 1lt cups vegetable or chicken stock
- 300g haggis
- Salt & pepper to taste

Method

1 Gently heat the olive oil in a large non-stick saucepan and sauté the vegetables for a few minutes until softened.

2 Add the stock and simmer for 5 minutes. Add the haggis and cook for a further 10 minutes or until everything is tender and cooked through.

3 Check the seasoning, divide into bowls and serve.

CHEF'S NOTE
If you've never tried haggis before this is a fab introduction. Another lovely recipe is haggis toasties with cheese and sweet chilli jam.

Bacon & Borlotti Soup

Ingredients

- 1 tbsp olive oil
- 1 onion, sliced
- 2 garlic cloves, crushed
- 2 slices of bacon, finely chopped
- 2 tbsp tomato puree
- 1.25lt chicken stock
- 1 tin borlotti beans, drained
- Salt & pepper to taste

Method

1 Gently sauté the onion, garlic & bacon in a large non-stick saucepan with the olive oil until the onions are softened and the bacon is cooked.

2 Stir through the tomato puree, add the stock & beans and simmer for 8 minutes.

3 Use the back of a large spoon or fork to crush some of the beans against the side of the pan. Combine well and cook for a further 5 minutes or until everything is piping hot.

4 Check the seasoning and serve.

CHEF'S NOTE
Crushing some of the beans will give the soup a chunky base, or you could blend a couple of ladles and return to the pan for a smoother base.

SERVES 4

Chinese Pork & Pak Choi

SUPER SIMPLE

.... Ingredients ....

- 300g rice
- 500g/14oz pork mince
- 1 onion, chopped
- 1 egg
- 1 tbsp olive
- 3 garlic cloves, crushed

- 1 large pinch chilli flakes
- 1 tbsp lime juice
- 1 tsp ground ginger
- 2 tbsp sweet chilli sauce
- 2 Pak Choi, shredded
- Salt & pepper to taste

.... Method ....

1 Cook the rice in a pan of salted boiling until tender. Drain when ready.

2 Meanwhile use a mixer to combine together the pork, onions, egg, garlic, chilli flakes, lime juice & ginger.

3 Use your hands to form the meatball mixture into firm walnut sized balls.

4 Heat the olive oil in a non-stick frying pan and stir-fry for 8-12 minutes or until the balls are cooked through and piping hot.

5 Place them on a chopping board and quarter, return to the pan with the rice, Pak Choi and sweet chilli sauce (add a little more oil if needed)

6 Stir-fry for a minute or two long and serve.

CHEF'S NOTE
Make sure the meatball mixture is pressed together firmly as they need to hold together while you are stir-frying them in the pan.

43

Mustard Chicken & Soya Bean Salad

Ingredients

- 6 boneless chicken thighs
- 2 tbsp Dijon mustard
- 3 tbsp olive oil
- ½ tsp chilli flakes
- 1 bunch fresh basil, chopped
- 300g/11oz frozen soya beans
- 1 red onion, very finely sliced
- Salt & pepper to taste

Method

1 Pre-heat the grill.

2 Cook the soya beans in salted boiling water until tender, drain and put to one side.

3 Season the chicken and cook under the grill for 10-15 minutes or until cooked through.

4 Place on a chopping board and slice into strips. Place in a bowl with the mustard, combine well and put back under the grill for a minute or two.

5 Meanwhile toss together the olive oil, chillies, basil, beans, cooked soya beans and sliced red onion.

6 Divide into bowls and serve the warm mustard chicken slices over the cool bean salad.

CHEF'S NOTE
Frozen soya beans are a fab budget ingredient, they are also referred to as soy beans and edamame.

The Classic Burger

SUPER SIMPLE

Ingredients

- 450g beef mince
- 1 tbsp olive oil
- 2 garlic cloves, crushed
- 1 tsp tomato ketchup
- 1 tsp mustard
- 1 egg, lightly beaten

- 1 pinch paprika
- 1 onion, sliced
- 1 tbsp Worcestershire sauce
- 4 burger rolls
- Handful of salad leaves
- 1 large tomatoes, sliced

Method

1 In a large bowl, mix together the mince, garlic, tomato ketchup, mustard, egg, paprika.

2 Use you hands to combine really well before forming into four patties.

3 Heat a little olive oil in a large non-stick frying pan and fry the burgers for 5–6 minutes each side or until cooked through.

4 Serve in burger buns with salad.

CHEF'S NOTE
Nothing beats a good burger. If you want to reduce the cost a bit; reduce the meat and add a coupe of slices worth of breadcrumbs to bulk it up.

SUPER
SIMPLE

One Pound
NON MEAT/VEGGIE
Recipes

Spicy Miso Soup

Ingredients

- 2 garlic cloves, crushed
- 1 tsp crushed
- ½ tsp ground ginger
- 4 tbsp miso paste
- 1.25lt boiling water
- 1 Pak Choi shredded
- 200g thin egg noodles
- Salt & pepper to taste

Method

1 Add the water and miso paste to a non-stick saucepan and stir well on a medium heat.

2 Add all the ingredients to the pan and cook for 3-4 minutes or until everything is cooked through and piping hot.

3 Check the seasoning, spoon into bowls and serve.

4 Quick and easy, you can add almost any vegetables or shredded meat you like.

CHEF'S NOTE
Miso packs a fantastic flavour punch in this simple soup.

Garlic & Samphire Gnocchi

SUPER SIMPLE

Ingredients

- 1 onion, chopped
- 2 garlic cloves, crushed
- 3 tbsp butter

- 500g fresh gnocchi
- 120g samphire
- 1 tbsp grated Parmesan style cheese

Method

1 Gently sauté the onions and garlic in the butter for a few minutes until softened.

2 Cook the gnocchi in salted boiling water, adding the samphire for the last 30 seconds of cooking.

3 Drain and add to the frying pan with the buttery onions.

4 Combine well and serve straight away with the Parmesan sprinkled over the top.

CHEF'S NOTE

Samphire, a relative of the parsley family, grows on rocks and cliffs by the sea. You'll need to go to some of the bigger supermarkets to find it in the fresh vegetable/herb aisle.

Nasi Goreng

Ingredients

- 8 tbsp olive oil
- 4 onions, sliced
- 8 garlic cloves, crushed
- 1 savoy cabbage, shredded
- 350g cooked brown rice
- 4 tbsp soy sauce
- 1-2 tsp chilli flakes
- 4 eggs

Method

1 Cook the rice in salted boiling water until tender, then drain.

2 Meanwhile heat the oil in a wok, add the onions & garlic and cook for a few minutes until slightly tender.

3 Add the cabbage and cook for a couple of minutes.

4 Add the drained rice, soy sauce and chilli flakes.

5 Make four holes in the rice to fry the eggs in.

6 Crack an egg in each hole until the eggs are fried and ready to eat.

7 Serve the rice in shallow bowls, topped with the fried egg.

CHEF'S NOTE
Serve with more soy sauce and chilli flakes if you like.

Veggie 'Pizzas'

SUPER SIMPLE

Ingredients

- 4 tbsp passata
- 4 flatbreads or large pitta breads
- 1 tsp mixed herbs
- 2 handfuls spinach, chopped
- 1 garlic clove, chopped
- 4 handfuls of grated cheese
- 4 eggs

Method

1 Heat the oven to 180C/Gas5.

2 Spread the passata over each flatbread.

3 Scatter the spinach, herbs and grated cheese over the top.

4 Crack an egg onto the centre of each flat bread.

5 Bake for around 10 mins or until the cheese has melted and the egg is cooked to your liking.

6 Season and serve.

CHEF'S NOTE
Add whichever toppings you like to these simple 'pizzas'.

Veggie Ramen

Ingredients

- 1 lt vegetable stock
- 2 tbsp teriyaki sauce
- 1 tbsp olive oil
- 200g mushrooms, sliced

- 1 onion, sliced
- 250g dried egg noodles
- 1 bag shredded mixed greens

Method

1 Dissolve the teriyaki sauce in a pan with the simmering stock.

2 Meanwhile gently sauté the mushrooms and onions in the olive oil for a few minutes.

3 Add the noodles to the stock and when the mushrooms are tender, add these along with the shredded greens.

4 Make sure everything is tender, check the seasoning and serve.

CHEF'S NOTE
Don't worry about having left over teriyaki sauce. It keeps well in the fridge and there are multiple other recipes to make use of it in this book.

Mushroom Puff Tart

SUPER SIMPLE

Ingredients

- 250g ready made puff pastry
- 2 tbsp olive oil
- 500g mushroom

- 2 garlic cloves, crushed
- 250g tub ricotta
- Bag of rocket

Method

1 Pre-heat the oven to 220C/Gas 7.

2 Roll the puff pastry out into a square measuring approx. 35x25cm on a piece of baking parchment.

3 Place the pastry and parchment on a baking sheet and cook for 10-15 mins.

4 Meanwhile gently sauté the garlic in the oil for a minute or two before adding the mushrooms and cooking until the mushrooms until softened.

5 Remove the pastry from the oven and drain and divide the mushrooms over the top.

6 Dollop the ricotta in small dots on top of the mushrooms and place back in the oven for another 5-10 minutes.

7 Remove the tart from the oven. Quarter the pastry, place on plates and heap the rocket on top.

CHEF'S NOTE
A block of puff pastry works out cheaper than a pre-rolled sheet.

Baked Potatoes With A Twist

Ingredients

- 4 large sweet potatoes
- 1 tin tuna
- 1 red onion, thinly sliced
- Pinch chilli flakes
- 1 lime
- Small tub plain Greek yoghurt

Method

1 Pierce the sweet potatoes a few times with a fork.

2 Place in the microwave and cook for about 15-20 mins, or until tender.

3 Split each sweet potato in half lengthways and place two halves on each of the 4 plates (cut-side up)

4 Flake the tuna with a fork and scatter over the sweet potato halves.

5 Top with sliced red onion a pinch of chilli and a dollop of Greek yoghurt.

6 Serve with a quarter of lime on the side of each plate to squeeze over when eating.

CHEF'S NOTE
This makes a fab quick and easy weekend lunch for the family.

Aubergine Curry

SUPER SIMPLE

Ingredients

- 2-3 aubergines
- 3 tbsp olive oil
- 1 tsp sugar
- 2 onions
- 2 garlic cloves, crushed
- 2 tbsp curry powder
- 1 tin chopped tomatoes
- 1 tin coconut milk

Method

1 Pre-heat the oven to 200F/Gas 6.

2 Slice the aubergines into rounds (or chunks if you prefer) and combine with 2 tbsp of the olive oil and the sugar.

3 Season with plenty of salt & pepper. Place on a baking tray and roast for 20 mins or until softened and golden.

4 Meanwhile sauté the onion and garlic in the remaining olive oil until softened.

5 Add the curry powder, stir well for a minute or two then add the tinned tomatoes, coconut milk and roasted aubergines.

6 Bring the coconut milk to a gentle simmer before covering with a lid (or plate) and leaving to simmer for 15-20 minutes.

7 Check the seasoning and serve.

CHEF'S NOTE
Serve with some ready make roti or chapattis. You can pick up a packet of 6 in most supermarkets for 75p or less.

Sunshine Hash

Ingredients

- 850g potatoes, cut into medium chunks
- 1 tbsp butter
- 4 eggs
- Pinch chilli flakes (use you discretion to suit your family's tastes)
- 260g tinned pineapple chunks (drained weight)

Method

1 Boil the potatoes in salted water for 7-10 minutes until just tender.

2 Gently warm the butter in a frying pan. Add the potatoes and chilli and fry over a medium heat for 10-12 mins moving the potatoes around the pan from time to time.

3 Add the pineapple and cook for another 5 minutes.

4 Crack the eggs into the pan evenly so that you have got an egg in each quarter of the pan.

5 Cover with a lid (or a plate is fine) and cook for about 5-8 mins over a medium heat until the eggs are cooked to your liking and everything is piping hot.

6 Season with salt & pepper, dish up into shallow bowls and serve.

CHEF'S NOTE

If you have any fresh green herbs like basil or coriander around feel free to add as garnish. Also a couple of rashers of any leftover bacon or ham will make a good addition.

Marmite Spaghetti & Pangritata

SUPER SIMPLE

Ingredients

- 350g Spaghetti/linguine or whatever pasta you have in the cupboard
- 2 tsp marmite
- 1 tbsp butter
- 3 slices bread
- 3 tbsp olive oil
- 2 garlic cloves, crushed

Method

1 Cook the pasta in salted boiling water until tender.

2 Whilst the pasta is cooking whizz the bread in a food processor to make breadcrumbs.

3 Warm the olive oil in a frying pan and gently sauté the garlic.

4 After a minute or two tip the breadcrumbs into the oil. Increase the heat and fry until all the oil is absorbed and the breadcrumbs are nice and crispy.

5 Tip the crispy breadcrumbs out onto a plate with some kitchen roll to cool.

6 When the pasta is cooked, drain, return to the pan and stir through the butter and marmite until really well combined.

7 Divide into shallow bowls and sprinkle the breadcrumbs over the top to serve.

CHEF'S NOTE
Pangritata was traditionally used in Italy as a substitute for Parmesan when money was tight - This tasty meal will cost you pennies rather than pounds.

Crunchy Fresh Tabbouleh

Ingredients

- 6 tbsp olive oil
- 1 tbsp curry powder
- 2 tins chickpeas, drained and rinsed
- 200g couscous
- 250g frozen peas

- 1 lemon
- 1 bunch fresh mint, finely chopped
- 200g radishes, roughly chopped
- 1 cucumber, chopped

Method

1 Pre-heat the oven to 200C/Gas 6.

2 Toss 3 tbsp of the oil with the chickpeas and curry powder.

3 Place the chickpeas on a baking tray and cook in the oven for 15 mins until they start to crisp a little.

4 Meanwhile cook the couscous, fluff with a fork and put to one side. Also cook the peas and put to one side.

5 When the chickpeas are ready, place in a large bowl with the couscous, peas, mint, radishes, cucumber and the rest of the olive oil.

6 Divide into bowls and serve with a lemon quarter on the side.

CHEF'S NOTE
Couscous is a great budget ingredient. Try buying whole-wheat couscous. You can pick up a large packet that will be enough for multiple recipes for 70p or less.

Tofu Laksa

SUPER SIMPLE

Ingredients

- 1 onion
- 2 garlic cloves
- 1 tbsp tomato puree
- 1 tbsp ground curry powder

- 1 tbsp tamarind paste
- 1 tin chopped tomatoes
- 1 tsp, chilli flakes
- 1 tbsp olive oil
- 500ml vegetable stock

- 1 tin coconut milk
- 2 tbsp soy sauce
- 125g tofu, cubed
- 200g thin egg noodles
- Salt & pepper to taste

Method

1 Place the onions, garlic cloves, lemon, tomato puree, tamarind paste, tomatoes & chilli in a food processor and pulse until finely chopped into a fresh paste.

2 Using the olive oil sauté the paste in a large non-stick saucepan for 5 minutes.

3 Add the rest of the ingredients and simmer for 3-5 minutes or until everything is cooked through and piping hot.

4 Check the seasoning and serve.

CHEF'S NOTE
Try serving with some freshly chopped chilli or lime wedges.

Eggs Turkish Style

Ingredients

- 2 tbsp olive oil
- 2 onions, sliced
- 2 red peppers, deseeded & sliced
- 2 garlic cloves, crushed
- 1 tin chopped tomatoes
- 2 tsp sugar
- 4 eggs
- Small tub sour cream
- 1 tsp paprika

Method

1 Gently sauté the onions, pepper & garlic in a frying pan with the olive oil.

2 Add the tomatoes and sugar and gently simmer.

3 Make four wells in the tomatoes in each corner of the pan and break the eggs in each well.

4 Cover the pan and cook for a few minutes more until the eggs are set.

5 Carefully split the pan into four and load into shallow bowls.

6 Dollop sour cream over the top and sprinkle a dusting of paprika over the top.

CHEF'S NOTE
Feel free to substitute the sour cream with Greek yogurt or crème fraiche.

Buttery Nut Couscous

SUPER SIMPLE

Ingredients

- 2 tbsp olive oil
- 1 onion, sliced
- 2 garlic cloves, crushed
- 200g frozen peas

- 600ml vegetable stock
- 400g couscous
- 2 tbsp peanut butter
- 1 tsp curry powder

Method

1 Heat oil in a saucepan over medium heat.

2 Add the onion, garlic & peas and cook for a few minutes.

3 Add the hot stock and bring to the boil.

4 Whisk in the peanut butter and curry power and tip in the couscous.

5 Combine well, remove from the heat and cover.

6 Allow it to sit for about 5 mins until all the stock is absorbed.

7 Fluff with a fork and serve.

CHEF'S NOTE
If you've got any leftover fresh herbs to hand sprinkle them over the top.

Feta & Walnut Wild Rice

Ingredients

- 350g brown rice
- 150g curly kale
- 75g walnuts, chopped
- 100g feta cheese, crumbled
- 1 tbsp olive oil

Method

1 Cook the rice in salted boiling water.

2 Meanwhile trim any thick stalks off the kale, chop and steam for a few minutes.

3 When the rice is ready drain and toss together with the kale, walnuts, feta and olive oil.

4 Season well and serve.

CHEF'S NOTE
Feel free to use Greek style salad cheese rather than feta – it can sometimes be as much as 50% cheaper.

Sweet Potato & Tomato Salad

SUPER SIMPLE

······· *Ingredients* ·······

- 2 tbsp olive oil
- 4 large sweet potatoes
- 240g of rocket/watercress/spinach leaves

- 750g tomatoes
- 100g Greek style cheese or Feta cheese

······· *Method* ·······

1 Pre-heat the oven to 200C/Gas 6.

2 Cube the sweet potatoes and toss with 1 tbsp of the olive oil and a little salt.

3 Place in the oven on a baking tray and roast for approx. 20 minutes or until they are crispy on the outside and tender on the inside.

4 Quarter the tomatoes and dice the feta cheese.

5 Assemble the salad leaves on plates with the roasted sweet potatoes, tomatoes and feta. Drizzle the remaining olive oil over the top and serve.

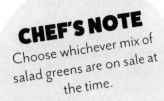

CHEF'S NOTE
Choose whichever mix of salad greens are on sale at the time.

Superfast Egg & Chutney Naans

Ingredients

- 8 eggs
- 1 small tub Greek yoghurt
- 4 large plain naan breads

- 4 tbsp mango chutney
- Pinch of chilli flakes
- Bunch of fresh coriander, chopped

Method

1 Fill a pan with boiling water. Reduce to a gentle simmer and carefully lower in the eggs.

2 Leave to simmer for 7minutes then drain.

3 Meanwhile take your naans, place on four plates and smother the mango chutney across the bread. Add a dollop of yoghurt on top.

4 Peel the eggs and sit these on the bread (two on each).

5 Cut the eggs in half then sprinkle with chilli flakes and fresh coriander to serve.

CHEF'S NOTE
You could easily make this simple recipe with pitta bread too...or toast some ordinary bread – delicious !!

Egg Molee

SUPER SIMPLE

Ingredients

- 300g rice
- 8 eggs
- 1 onion, chopped
- 1 tbsp olive oil

- 1 tin coconut milk
- 1 tin chopped tomatoes
- 2 tbsp curry powder

Method

1 Hard boil the eggs. Peel and cut in half.

2 Using a frying pan gently sauté the onions in the olive oil until golden.

3 Add the tomatoes and coconut milk to the onions along with the curry power. Combine well and warm through.

4 Add the hard boiled eggs, with the yolks facing upwards, cover and leave to gently cook

5 Meanwhile put the rice on to cook in salted boiling water.

6 When it's tender drain and serve with the eggs and tomatoes piled on top.

CHEF'S NOTE
In many parts of India fish and meat are rarely used in curries as they are expensive. More often eggs and lentils form the staple ingredients.

Spinach Spicy Lentils

Ingredients

- 300g rice
- 150g dried red split lentils
- 2 tbsp olive oil

- 2 onion, sliced
- 2 tbsp curry powder
- 1 bag spinach, chopped

Method

1 Cook the rice and lentils in separate pans according to the packet instructions.

2 Meanwhile heat the oil in a deep frying pan (or wok) and gently sauté the onions for a few minutes.

3 When they are softened and golden stir through the curry powder and cook for another couple of minutes to release the spices.

4 Drain the rice & lentils and add to the onions along with the spinach.

5 Heat through, toss really well and serve in bowls.

CHEF'S NOTE
Dried lentils are super cheap but precooked lentils are fine to use too. Just add to the pan along with the drained rice and heat through.

Halloumi Brioche Burgers

SUPER SIMPLE

.... *Ingredients* ....

- 225g/250g block halloumi cheese, cut into 8 thick slices
- 1 tsp olive oil
- 4 brioche buns
- 4 tbsp houmous
- 2 large tomatoes, sliced
- 1 red onion, sliced
- 1 iceberg lettuce shredded

.... *Method* ....

1 Warm a non stick frying pan and fry the halloumi slices in the oil for a couple of minutes each side.

2 Meanwhile assemble the tomatoes, lettuce, red onions and a dollop of houmous in each brioche bun.

3 When the cheese is ready, load two slices into each roll and serve.

CHEF'S NOTE
Halloumi cheese is a salty cheesy wonder-ingredient. It's great with a kick of chilli too if you want to add a few flakes.

Bombay Potatoes With Fresh Mint Raita

Ingredients

- 1kg potatoes, peeled and cut into small cubes
- 3 tbsp olive oil
- 200g frozen peas

- 250ml tub of plain yoghurt
- ½ cucumber, finely diced
- 1 bunch fresh mint, finely chopped
- 2 tbsp curry powder

Method

1 Bring the potatoes to the boil in salted water.

2 Simmer for 5-8 mins, or until tender. Drain and allow to steam dry for a few mins (adding the peas for the last couple of minutes of cooking).

3 While the potatoes are cooking make the raita by combining together the yoghurt, cucumber & mint and place in a serving bowl with a spoon.

4 Next, heat the olive oil in a frying pan and add the peas & potatoes.

5 Stir through the curry powder and gently fry for 5-10 mins or until golden.

6 Season well before serving in bowls with the raita placed on the table for everyone to help themselves.

CHEF'S NOTE
Add some chilli flakes to the potatoes if you wish. The raita will cool your mouth down nicely.

'Steaks' With Fresh Chimichurri

SUPER SIMPLE

········· *Ingredients* ·········

For the steaks:
- 2 heads cauliflower, sliced through core into 4 'steaks'
- 4 tbsp olive oil
- 1 tbsp paprika
- 4 cloves garlic, minced

For the chimichurri:
- 1 pack fresh coriander (or basil if you prefer)
- 1 pack flat-leaf parsley
- 2 garlic cloves
- 1 small onion

- 1 pinch chilli flakes
- 6 tbsp olive oil
- 1 tbsp red wine vinegar

········· *Method* ·········

1 Pre-heat the oven to 200C/Gas 6.

2 First combine together the olive oil, paprika and garlic. Season well, brush the cauliflower steaks with the oil and place in a single layer across one or two baking trays.

3 Roast for 20 minutes, take out of the oven, turn each steak over, brush with a little more oil then roast for another 15 mins or until tender.

4 While the steaks are roasting make the chimichurri by blitzing together all the chimichurri ingredients. Season well; you may need to adjust the balance of flavour to suit your own taste.

5 Serve the steaks with the chimichurri piled over the top.

CHEF'S NOTE
This is a great vegan option if you fancy going meat-free for a night.

Crunchy Blue Cheese Salad

Ingredients

- 5 tbsp red wine vinegar
- 2 tbsp olive oil
- 1 tbsp honey
- 1 tbsp Dijon mustard
- 4 apples cored & diced
- 1 large cauliflower
- 200g blue cheese, crumbled
- 50g walnuts, chopped

Method

1 Chop the cauliflower into small pieces.

2 Make the dressing by combining together the vinegar, oil, honey & mustard. Season well and check the balance of ingredients.

3 Toss the dressing in a bowl with the cauliflower, apple and walnuts.

4 Divide onto plates and pile the crumbled blue cheese over the top.

CHEF'S NOTE
Fresh, crunchy and delicious and ready to serve as a light lunch in minutes.

Sweet Potato Quesadillas

SUPER SIMPLE

Ingredients

- 600g sweet potatoes, peeled & diced
- 2 tbsp olive oil
- 100g feta cheese (or Greek style cheese), crumbled
- 1 big bag salad
- 8 small flour tortillas
- 1 small tub Greek yoghurt
- 2 tsp paprika

Method

1 Pre-heat the oven to 200C/Gas 6.

2 Boil the diced potatoes for 10 mins in salted water or until tender.

3 Drain, roughly smash with the back of a fork and put to one side.

4 Lay the tortillas out on baking tray(s) and load the potatoes & crumbled feta into the centre of each wrap along with some of the salad.

5 Fold each tortilla into quarters and push down with the heel of your hand to hold them together.

6 Drizzle with olive oil and bake in the oven for 10 mins until golden

7 Meanwhile mix together the yoghurt and paprika.

8 When the quesadillas are ready divide onto plates with the rest of the salad and a dollop of paprika yoghurt.

CHEF'S NOTE
You could also use butternut squash in these tasty quesadillas.

Tamarind & Squash Bloomer

········· **Ingredients** ·········

- 400g butternut squash, peeled & chopped
- 2 tbsp olive oil
- 4 tbsp tamarind paste
- Large pinch chilli flakes

- 2 tbsp butter (more if needed)
- 8 thick slices of a 'bloomer' loaf
- 100g grated cheese
- Small bag rocket

········· **Method** ·········

1 Pre-heat oven to 180C/Gas 5.

2 Combine the butternut squash with the olive oil, chilli flakes and tamarind paste.

3 Toss well, place on a baking tray and roast in the oven for 40 mins, or until tender.

4 Butter the bloomer slicers.

5 Pile the roasted squash, grated cheese and rocket onto 4 slices and close the sandwiches with the other 4 slices.

6 Push the tops right down to hold the sandwiches together & serve.

CHEF'S NOTE
If you have a sandwich toaster use it to quickly grill & press each bloomer for a couple of minutes.

Butternut Squash Macaroni Cheese

SUPER SIMPLE

Ingredients

- 400g butternut squash, deseeded & chopped
- 1 tbsp olive oil
- 400g macaroni
- 85g butter

- 85g plain flour
- 2 tsp Dijon mustard
- 750ml milk
- 150g cheddar cheese, grated

Method

1 Pre-heat the oven to 200C/Gas 7.

2 Toss the squash and oil together and cook for 20mins or until tender.

3 Towards the end of the roasting time begin cooking the macaroni in salted boiling water until tender.

4 While the pasta is cooking, gently warm a saucepan and melt the butter.

5 Stir through the flour to make a roux then gradually add the milk and mustard; whisking all the time with a balloon whisk.

6 Bring to the boil and gently simmer, whisking out any lumps as the sauce thickens.

7 Remove from the heat and add the cheese.

8 Combine together the cooked macaroni, squash & sauce and place in the hot oven for a further 15 minutes or until golden and bubbling.

CHEF'S NOTE
Breadcrumbs scattered over the top before the final spell in the oven adds a nice touch as does a pinch of ground nutmeg in the cheese sauce if you have it in the cupboard.

Classic Cauliflower Cheese

Ingredients

- 2 slices bread
- 2 garlic cloves
- 2 cauliflower heads, broken into pieces
- 1lt milk

- 8 tbsp flour
- 100g butter
- 200g grated cheddar cheese (or whichever cheese you have to hand)
- 1 tsp paprika

Method

1 Use a food processor to whizz the bread (along with the garlic cloves) into breadcrumbs.

2 Pre-heat the oven to 200C/Gas 7.

3 Steam the cauliflower pieces until tender.

4 Meanwhile gently warm a saucepan and melt the butter.

5 Stir through the flour to make a roux then gradually add the milk; whisking all the time with a balloon whisk.

6 Bring to the boil and gently simmer as you whisk out any lumps as the sauce thickens.

7 Remove from the heat and add the cheese. Load the cauliflower into a baking dish. Pour over the cheese sauce, sprinkle with the garlic breadcrumbs and a dusting of paprika.

8 Put in the oven and bake for 20 mins or until golden & bubbling.

CHEF'S NOTE
Cauliflower is not always a family favourite but this recipe helps get it onto the table in a tasty way which should appeal to everyone.

Fresh Herb Quinoa

SUPER SIMPLE

Ingredients

- 250g quinoa
- 1 vegetable stock cube
- Juice of 1 lemon
- 1 bunch spring onions, chopped
- 1 bunch fresh mint, chopped
- 1 bunch fresh flat leaf parsley, chopped
- ½ cucumber, deseeded and diced
- 4 tbsp olive oil

Method

1 Rinse the quinoa well and place in a pan with double the volume of water and a stock cube cubed in.

2 Bring to the boil, cover, reduce the heat and gently simmer for 10 mins or until tender.

3 Drain off any remaining liquid.

4 Use a fork to flush the quinoa and leave to cool for a few minutes.

5 Stir in the lemon juice, chopped herbs, spring onions, cucumber and oil and serve.

CHEF'S NOTE
Quinoa has become really popular over the past few years. It makes a great alternative to rice and pasta.

Halloumi & Watermelon Rice

Ingredients

- 300g rice
- 1 vegetable stock cube
- 1-2 tbsp olive
- 1 cucumber, cubed

- 250g halloumi cheese, cut into 10-12 slices
- Zest and juice 1 lemon
- ¼ watermelon, cut into small cubes

Method

1 Cook the rice in boiling water, along with the crumbled stock cube, until tender. Drain and put to one side to cool.

2 Heat a drizzle of oil in a non stick frying pan. Add the halloumi slices and fry for 2-3 mins on each side or until golden.

3 Toss the remaining oil, cucumber, lemon zest and juice with the rice.

4 Divide into shallow bowls. Arrange the halloumi and watermelon pieces on top and serve.

CHEF'S NOTE
You could substitute the rice for pasta, quinoa or pearl barley if you prefer or have store cupboard supplies to use up.

Fresh Basil Orzo

SUPER SIMPLE

Ingredients

- 350g orzo
- 1lt vegetable stock (more if needed)
- 1 tbsp olive oil
- 1 garlic clove, crushed
- 1 onion, chopped
- Juice of 1 lemon
- 1 bunch fresh basil, chopped
- 4 tbsp Parmesan style hard cheese, grated

Method

1 Cook the orzo in the stock per the packet instructions (add some more water if needed) until tender.

2 Meanwhile gently sauté the garlic and onions in the olive oil until softened.

3 When the orzo is ready, drain and tip into the pan with oily onions, juice of 1 lemon and fresh basil.

4 Combine well and add a little more oil if you need to loosen it up.

5 Divide into bowls and cover with the grated cheese.

CHEF'S NOTE
Orzo is tiny dried pasta which has a rice-like consistency. It sounds expensive but you can actually pick up a 500g packet for as little as 65p.

Baked Blue Cheese Gnocchi

Ingredients

- 2 slices bread
- 1 garlic clove
- 500g fresh gnocchi

- 200g frozen peas
- 2 tbsp crème fraiche
- 125g soft blue cheese

Method

1 First whizz the bread and garlic in a food processor to make breadcrumbs.

2 Pre-heat the grill.

3 Cook the gnocchi in salted boiling water, adding the peas for the last minute or two of cooking.

4 Drain, return to the pan and stir through the crème fraiche and blue cheese.

5 Load into a baking dish. Sprinkle the breadcrumbs on top with plenty of seasoning.

6 Place the dish under a hot grill until the cheese is bubbling and golden.

7 Serve immediately.

CHEF'S NOTE
Just go for whichever type of blue cheese is on sale at the time.

Beetroot & Horseradish Soup

SUPER SIMPLE

Ingredients

- 1 tbsp olive oil
- 1 onion, sliced
- 600g cooked beetroot, chopped
- 1lt vegetable stock

- 4 tbsp Greek yogurt
- 1 tbsp horseradish sauce
- Salt & pepper to taste

Method

1 Gently heat the olive oil in a large non-stick saucepan and sauté the onions for a few minutes until softened.

2 Add the beetroot & stock and simmer for 5-6 minutes or until everything is cooked through and piping hot.

3 Tip the soup into a blender or food processor along with the yogurt & horseradish sauce and whizz until you have a completely smooth texture.

4 Check the seasoning and serve.

CHEF'S NOTE
Adjust the quantity of horseradish to suit your own taste.

Tofu & Coriander Bowl

Ingredients

For the tofu
- 2 tbsp olive oil
- 400g firm fresh tofu, drained and cubed
- 4 tbsp soy sauce

- 1 tbsp balsamic vinegar

For the beans
- 1 tbsp olive oil
- 1 tsp chilli flakes
- 200g frozen soya beans,

defrosted
- 1 tbsp soy sauce
- 1 tsp balsamic vinegar
- 1 bunch fresh coriander, finely chopped

Method

1 First make the tofu by heating the olive oil in a large frying pan and cook the cubed tofu for a couple of minutes. Add the soy sauce & balsamic vinegar and cook until the tofu is browned on each side and the soy sauce has reduced right down. Tip the tofu out and put to one side.

2 In the meantime heat the rest of the oil in another frying pan and stir-fry the chilli and beans together along with the soy and vinegar.

3 Quickly combine together the beans and tofu in a single pan, divide into bowls and sprinkle with lots of fresh coriander to serve.

CHEF'S NOTE
Tofu is a versatile vegan ingredient which takes on the flavour of sauces really well.

Kale & Mushroom Supper

SUPER SIMPLE

Ingredients

- 2 tbsp olive oil
- 300g mushrooms, sliced
- 2 garlic cloves, crushed
- Large bag kale

- 2 tsp Worcestershire sauce
- 4 eggs
- Salt & pepper

Method

1 Heat the olive oil in a large non-stick frying pan. Sauté the mushrooms and garlic for a few minutes.

2 Finely chop the kale (removing any thick stalks) and add to the pan along with the Worcestershire sauce.

3 Once all the kale has wilted, season well with lots of salt and pepper.

4 Crack in the eggs, cover the pan and leave to cook until the eggs are set.

5 Check the seasoning and serve.

CHEF'S NOTE
Spinach works just as well in this veggie supper.

Veggie 'Kedgeree'

Ingredients

- 350g Rice
- 4 eggs
- 1 olive oil
- 1 onion,

- 1 red pepper
- 2 tbsp curry power
- 100g frozen peas,
- 1 small tub crème fraiche

Method

1 Cook the rice in salted boiling water until tender, then drain.

2 Hard boil the eggs for 6 minutes, leave to cool then peel.

3 Meanwhile, heat the oil in a large frying pan and sauté the onions, peppers & peas for a few minutes.

4 Add the drained rice and curry powder. Cook for a couple of minutes until everything is cooked through and piping hot.

5 Stir through the crème fraiche until warmed.

6 Divide into bowls. Quarter the eggs and add to each bowl to serve.

CHEF'S NOTE
Including any leftover veggies in the fridge makes this the ultimate budget busting dish.

SUPER SIMPLE

One Pound
FISH
Recipes

Smoked Fish & Borlotti Beans

················· **Ingredients** ·················

- 250g frozen smoked haddock fillets
- 500ml chicken stock
- 2 tins borlotti beans, drained & rinsed
- 1 tbsp olive oil
- 1 bunch flat leaf parsley, chopped
- 1 tbsp lemon juice
- Salt & pepper to taste

················· **Method** ·················

1 Heat the stock in a high-sided non-stick frying pan and gently poach the fish fillets until cooked through.

2 Leaving the poaching liquid in the pan remove the fish fillets, wrap them in foil to keep them warm and put to one side.

3 Add the drained borlotti beans to the poaching liquid and cook for 4-5 minutes until piping hot.

4 Drain the beans and return them to the empty pan. Flake the fish and add to the beans along with the oil, parsley and lemon juice.

5 Remove from the heat combine gently, season with lots of black pepper and serve.

CHEF'S NOTE
Frozen fillets tend to be the cheapest way to buy smoked fish. There's no particular reason to go for haddock, any firm white fish will do.

SERVES 4

Tuna Tart

SUPER SIMPLE

·········· *Ingredients* ··········

- 320g pack puff pastry
- 1 tin tuna
- 1 tin sweetcorn, drained

- 3 tbsp crème fraiche
- 1 tsp paprika
- Handful of cheddar cheese, grated

·········· *Method* ··········

1 Heat oven to 220C/Gas 7.

2 Lay the pastry out on a baking sheet lined with parchment.

3 Prick the pastry a couple of times and bake in the oven for 10 minutes.

4 Meanwhile combine together the tuna, sweetcorn, creme fraiche, paprika and cheese together with plenty of seasoning.

5 Remove the pastry from the oven, spread the tuna mix evenly over the top and return to the oven.

6 Bake for 10-15 mins more or until golden and cooked through.

7 Cut into quarters and serve.

CHEF'S NOTE
Don't worry if you don't have any crème fraiche just add a bit more cheese.

Crab Linguine

Ingredients

- 350g linguine
- 1 tbsp olive oil
- 2 garlic cloves, crushed
- 1 tin crab meat
- 1 small tub crème fraiche
- 1 lemon
- 1 bag rocket

Method

1 Cook the linguine in salted boiling water until tender.

2 Meanwhile gently sauté the garlic in the olive oil for a few minutes.

3 Stir in the crabmeat, a little lemon zest and the crème fraiche to gently warm through.

4 Add the drained pasta and toss.

5 Season and serve with the rocket piled on top and a lemon quarter on the side.

CHEF'S NOTE
Tinned crab meat is great value. A small tin can cost you less than £1.60 and it's just as good as fresh crabmeat.

Crab & Potato 'Samosas'

SUPER SIMPLE

······· *Ingredients* ·······

- 2 medium potatoes, cut into quarters
- 5 tbsp butter
- 1 onion, chopped
- 1 tin crabmeat
- 12 sheets filo pastry

······· *Method* ·······

1 Pre-heat the oven to 200C/Gas 6

2 Boil the potatoes in salted boiling water for 10-15 mins until tender.

3 Meanwhile, place the butter in a saucepan and melt.

4 Add the onions and cook for a couple of mins.

5 Meanwhile finely dice the cooked potatoes.

6 In a bowl combine together the diced potatoes, flaked crabmeat and buttery onions to form a tasty filling.

7 Brush melted butter over three sheets of filo pastry and lay on top of each other.

8 Cut the filo sheets lengthways into 3 long strips. Then cut each strip in half across the middle.

9 Place a teaspoon of the crab mixture onto the bottom right-hand corner of each filo strip. Fold the filo over to make a triangle, then fold again, rolling up the strip. When the mixture is enclosed and you have a neat triangle shape, place on a baking sheet and brush with more butter. Repeat with the remaining pastry sheets and filling.

10 Place in the oven and bake for 15-20 mins until golden and crisp.

Smoked Salmon Omelette

Ingredients

- 8 large eggs
- 1 onion, finely sliced
- Bunch of fresh chives, chopped
- 4 tsp butter
- 120g smoked salmon trimmings

Method

1 Break the eggs, whisk with a fork and add the finely chopped onions and fresh chives.

2 Heat a 1 tsp of butter in a non stick frying pan and add a quarter of the egg mixture.

3 Tilt the pan so the mixture covers the base and cook gently for 2-3 minutes or until almost set.

4 Add a quarter of the smoked salmon strips, fold the omelette and cook for another minute.

5 Keep it warm in the oven while you cook the remaining omelettes then dish up each as soon they're ready.

CHEF'S NOTE
Salmon trimmings are great value. You can pick up a 120g packet for as little as £1.65.

The Best Ever Egg Fried Rice

SUPER SIMPLE

Ingredients

- 400g rice
- 1 tbsp olive oil
- 3 tbsp sweet chilli sauce
- 4 eggs

- 1 packet silken tofu, cubed
- 100g frozen cooked prawns, defrosted & chopped

Method

1 Cook the rice in salted boiling water and drain.

2 Heat the oil in a large frying pan.

3 Add the cooked rice, sweet chilli sauce and prawns.

4 Move quickly around the pan before breaking in the eggs and adding the tofu.

5 Continue stir-frying until the everything is piping hot.

6 Check the seasoning and serve.

CHEF'S NOTE
You won't find silken tofu in the budget supermarkets but it's still an economical ingredient which adds a lovely creamy texture to this dish.

Fresh Creamy Mussels

Ingredients

- 1kg mussels in their shells, scrubbed & prepared
- 4 garlic cloves, crushed
- 1 tbsp olive oil
- 500ml vegetable stock
- 50ml single cream

Method

1 Gently sauté the garlic in the olive oil using deep pan.

2 After a few minutes add the stock and bring to the boil.

3 Add the mussels, cover and leave to cook for approx. 4 minutes.

4 Give the pan a shake while it's cooking and when the mussels open scoop them out into four bowls (discard any mussels which are not open).

5 Take the stock off the heat. Stir through the cream and tip this sauce over the mussels in the bowl.

6 Delicious and ready to serve.

CHEF'S NOTE
If you shop around supermarket fish counters you'll often see fresh mussels on sale...that's the time to try out this decadent dinner.

Prawn & Rice Soup Bowl

SUPER SIMPLE

Ingredients

- 200g rice
- 1 onion
- 1 tbsp olive oil
- 2 tbsp curry power

- 200g frozen prawns, defrosted & chopped
- 1 tin coconut milk

Method

1 Cook the rice in salted boiling water.

2 After 10 minutes begin sautéing the onions in a frying pan with the olive oil.

3 Stir in the curry powder and add the coconut milk. When it's warmed through add the chopped prawns.

4 Once the rice is ready, drain and add to the frying pan.

5 Cook until everything is piping hot.

6 Dish up in shallow bowls and serve straight away.

CHEF'S NOTE
Serve with some chunky crusty bread, if you have any, to mop of the coconut soupy sauce.

Indian Fish Wraps

Ingredients

- 2 tins sardines
- 1 tbsp olive oil
- 1 onion, sliced
- 1 tbsp curry powder

- 2 tbsp mango chutney
- Handful of lettuce or salad greens
- 4 chapattis or tortilla wraps

Method

1 Use a fork to mash the sardines in a bowl.

2 Heat the olive oil in a frying pan and gently sauté the onions for a few minutes until softened.

3 Add the curry powder and sardines. Combine really well for a couple of minutes to warm everything through.

4 Take off the heat, stir in the mango chutney.

5 Load onto the chapattis with the salad, fold to eat.

CHEF'S NOTE
Bulk up this meal with some tinned chickpeas too if you like. Just add these to the pan with the onions.

Angel Hair Anchovies

SUPER SIMPLE

Ingredients

- 350g angel hair pasta (any thin spaghetti will do the job)
- 1 tin anchovies
- 1 onion
- 2 tbsp olive oil

- ½ tsp chilli flakes
- 1 lemon
- 4 tbsp Parmesan/hard grated cheese

Method

1 Cook the pasta in salted boiling water.

2 Whilst the pasta is cooking, gently heat the olive oil in a frying pan and sauté the onions for a few minutes.

3 Add the anchovies and break up with a spoon so that they almost 'dissolve' into the oil.

4 Add the chilli flakes and cook for another couple of minutes.

5 When the pasta is ready, drain and toss with the anchovy steeped oil.

6 Serve with a lemon wedge on the side and Parmesan cheese over the top.

CHEF'S NOTE
Anchovies have a real depth making them great for adding flavour to simple dishes.

Sardine & Olive Pasta

Ingredients

- 350g spaghetti
- 1 tbsp olive oil
- 1 tin sardines in tomato sauce)
- 1 red onion, sliced
- 2 garlic cloves, crushed
- 10 black pitted olives, sliced
- Salt & pepper to taste

Method

1 Fill a saucepan with boiling water and a good pinch of salt. Add the pasta and leave to cook until the spaghetti is tender.

2 Meanwhile heat the olive oil in a high-sided non-stick frying pan and gently sauté the sardines, onions, garlic & olives for 10-15 minutes or until everything is cooked through and piping hot.

3 Drain the pasta and add to the sardine pan. Toss really well, divide into bowls and serve.

CHEF'S NOTE
This is a super easy store cupboard meal you can rustle up in minutes. If your budget can stretch to capers add a tbsp of chopped capers to the frying with the sardines.

Coconut Milk Chowder

SUPER SIMPLE

Ingredients

- 1 onion, chopped
- 1 pinch crushed chilli flakes
- 400g potatoes, peeled & cubed
- 1 tin sweet corn, drained
- 100g frozen peas
- 1lt hot chicken stock
- 200g frozen fish pie mix
- 1 tin coconut milk
- Salt & pepper to taste

Method

1 Gently simmer the onions, chilli, potatoes, sweetcorn & peas in the hot chicken stock for 8-10 minutes or until the potatoes are tender.

2 Add the fish pie mix & coconut milk and continue to cook for 3-5 minutes or until the prawns are cooked through.

3 Check the seasoning and serve.

CHEF'S NOTE
Frozen fish pie mix is a great budget option. Shop around; you can get a good deal for a couple of quid.

Simple Fish Stew With Couscous

.... **Ingredients** ....

- 1 tbsp olive oil
- 1 onion, chopped
- 2 garlic cloves, crushed
- 200g frozen fish pie mix
- 500ml tomato passata
- Pinch of dried crushed chillies
- ½ tsp each salt & brown sugar
- 200g couscous
- 370ml hot chicken stock
- Salt & pepper to taste

.... **Method** ....

1 Heat the oil in a non-stick frying pan and gently sauté the onion and garlic for a few minutes until softened.

2 Add the fish, passata, chillies, salt & sugar and cook for 10-15 minutes, stirring occasionally to encourage the fillets to break up a little.

3 Meanwhile place the boiling stock and couscous in a bowl. Cover and leave for 3-4 minutes or until the stock is absorbed. Fluff with a fork and divide into shallow bowls. Serve with the fish stew ladled over the top.

CHEF'S NOTE
You may need a little more salt/sugar to balance the acidity of the tomato passata.

Printed in Great Britain
by Amazon

84013661R00059